STATIC

life on

EDITORS: IAN DALEY AND JO HENDERSON
PHOTOGRAPHER: NICK MEEK

YORKSHIRE ART CIRCUS

1998

Published by Yorkshire Art Circus, School Lane, Glasshoughton, Castleford, West Yorkshire, WF10 4QH. Tel:01977 550401 Fax:01977 512819
e-mail: admin@artcircus.org.uk Web site: www.artcircus.org.uk

ISBN: 1 898311 37 4

Design: Martha Tullberg
Typesetting: Yorkshire Art Circus
Printing: FM Repro Ltd, Roberttown, Liversedge

Contributors: John Barras, Alfie Boswell, Kathleen Cawley, Alfie Conners, Joanne Connors, Anne Cunningham, Sharan Dunn, John Doran, Mary Doran, Joanne Eubank, Michael Eubank, Mary Flynn, Nelson Lee, Danny Lowther, Mary Lowther, Theresa Lowther, Philomena Lowther, Violet Lowther, Chanelle Nicholson, Ed Nicholson, Margaret Nicholson, Margaret P Nicholson, Marina Nicholson, Mudsy Nicholson, Rita Nicholson, Shirley Nicholson, John Price, Julie Price, Phillip Price, Roseanne Price, Bessie Smith, Crystal Smith, Mary Smith, plus several others who didn't want to be named in the book

Thanks to: Clare Conlon, David Day, John Eckart, Peter Elliott, Pam Gillon, Dave Harriman, Lorna Hey, Viv Hughes, Paula Love, Chris Meek, Peter Nightingale, Hughie Smith, Sue Todd, Steve Ullmand

British Library cataloguing in Publication Data
A catalogue record for this book is available from the British Library.

Yorkshire Art Circus is a unique book publisher. We work to increase access to writing and publishing and to develop new models of practice for the arts in the community. Please write to us for details of our full programme of workshops and our current book list.
Yorkshire Art Circus is a registered charity No 1007443

Yorkshire Art Circus is grateful for support for this book from Wakefield Community Education

Yorkshire Art Circus is supported by:

West Yorkshire Grants

Yorkshire & Humberside ARTS

City of Wakefield Metropolitan District Council
Leisure Services

FOREWORD

by sue todd

As members of the Traveller Education Team in Wakefield we have been privileged to work with the children and their families on the Heath Common Site and in doing so have been told many of the stories written here first hand. One of the aims of the Traveller Education Service is to build trust and understanding between the Traveller families, the schools and other agencies which we do by communicating the differences and similarities between people to both Travellers and to the wider community. Although there are obvious differences, there is a mutual respect for the basic values of family, community and education in its broadest sense and that is something that is common to all of us.

Initially the purpose of the book was to offer the Travellers on Wakefield site a vehicle for their thoughts, feelings and frustrations. When the book was first suggested, there was a lot of suspicion, because Travellers are not used to their words and stories being valued. However, since their culture is based around the story telling tradition, once people got started the stories flowed. As a result the book is full of images and reminiscences which demonstrate how Travellers have adapted and managed their lives during a time of great change. Their stories are fascinating, illuminating and moving and are a powerful record for the Travellers, their children, and for others outside their community. What comes through loud and clear is that they are unique and independent people and they are proud of their lifestyle and history. Their homes and their families are of paramount importance to them.

This book highlights the modern experience of Traveller families in the Wakefield district and acknowledges their ability to adapt. It also offers a unique opportunity for greater understanding of each other and what is important to all of us.

INTRODUCTION

by ian daley and jo henderson

During the planning stages of this book, we were asked many times what the book would be about. We would reply that it would contain images and stories about the Travellers on Heath Common Site.

'Yes, but what will it be about?'

'We can't possibly know.'

And that was the truth. We purposely approached the book with an open mind, we didn't read up excessively about the Traveller life, we were armed only with the notion that the Traveller culture was an oral tradition and information was passed on by story telling. We wanted to get on site and listen to the stories and write them down.

The first day we set foot on to the Heath Common site was an unforgettable experience. Enthused at the prospect of starting to meet the people who lived on the site, we casually strolled into culture shock. The difference in the lifestyles of the Traveller community and the settled community was real. Running parallel to this induction, the Travellers weren't expecting us, they didn't know who we were and they couldn't have cared less about being in a book. The welcome wasn't hostile but we were greeted with a deal of suspicion.

The suspicion was understandable. Who needs strangers coming to their doors asking for chats? Our line of approach didn't help us much to begin with either.

'What do you want to talk about?' We were asked.

'Oh, anything you want.' We replied with good intention.

With a few good introductions by Sue and Pam from the Traveller Education Service, we started to find our way and were invited into caravans for tea and chats, and sometimes biscuits. We got a real sense of community as one door opened to another and then another. The impact of the words spoken in the caravans during those times extended well beyond working hours. The suggestions expressed were vibrant and stayed in the front of the mind, recurring for the rest of the day and night and then sinking in. Wherever we would find ourselves we would babble out stories we had just been told. The stories we were told on such days you can read in the following pages.

The value of recording such voices became increasingly apparent as we grew to know Travellers. As a whole, the Travellers seem to put up with a lot, yet there is seldom an organised voice of complaint. To compare the pristine cleanliness inside the caravans and on individual plots to the general mess of the site, tells a story in itself. The site sometimes was in such a state as to be disturbing. On another level, as a distinctly different lifestyle, the Traveller life is of interest to the settled community, there is value in raising awareness of what Travellers have to put up with.

Accompanying the stories is a stunning collection of photographs taken by Nick Meek. The photographs and words are organised in three sections to tell an overall story of the pride that the Travellers feel about their heritage, the conflicts that they face and the site they live on. That such a project could be pulled together over a six month period is testimony to the support we received from Sue and Pam, Peter Elliott and all at the Yorkshire Art Circus.

The first day we went on site we said to each other that we would have fond memories of this book and that was before we even got started. If the purpose of this introduction is to outline what the book is about, then I suppose we will have to say that it contains images and stories about the Travellers on Heath Common site. You can read it for yourself.

BACKGROUND

The name Gypsy was coined to describe a group of nomadic tradesmen and musicians who had made their way from India via Asia, Russia and Europe to arrive on these shores in the 15th century. In Germany they were known as the Egyptians, as they had told the Germans they came from the Middle East and in those days the Middle East was known as Little Egypt. When they arrived in England, the name was shortened to Gypsy.

Marginalisation of the Gypsies can be recorded as far back as Henry VIII who made it a hanging offence to be a tinker. There was suspicion of 'the devilish practices of witchcraft and fortune telling' and up until the 17th century, legislation was passed which made it an offence for tinkers and Travellers to sell their wares. The situation gradually changed and by the 1750s Gypsies were able to travel freely, earning their living by trading and selling, making use of their traditional skills.

A stable relationship emerged between the Gypsies and the settled community. The Gypsies moved round the country in small family groups, following a seasonal calendar of planting, fruit picking, labouring, festivals and horse fairs. The traditional prejudices still existed but there existed a mutual interdependence; the Gypsies providing much needed labour, skills and services and the host community happy to provide stopping sites in return for that work. This seasonal pattern created an informal network of sites across the country and the network of work-related sites allowed Gypsies freedom of movement and a degree of autonomy and self reliance.

This was all changed by an act that was, ironically, not aimed at the travelling community at all, but at developers who were buying plots of land and turning them into caravan sites. The 1960 *Caravan Sites and Control of Development Act* set standards of provision - numbers of toilets, water provision, mains connections - that were beyond the reach of a large number of these informal, transient sites. Rather than face prosecution from the health authorities for substandard sites, farmers, pub landlords, private landowners, all of whom had been happy for Gypsies to use a side of the road or a strip of land out at the back, denied access to their traditional stopping areas, displacing large numbers of families and destroying the informal country-wide network. At about the same time, between 1962 and 1964, a large number of Irish Travellers came to England, driven out by pressure from the *Itinerant Settlers Committee* who were trying to get Travellers in Ireland settled into houses. The changing nature of agriculture - mechanization replacing labourers - as well as road and housing developments building over traditional sites, contributed to the disintegration of these traditional patterns and relationships.

As a partial response to the growing problem the Government passed the *1968 Caravan Act.* This made it the responsibility of county authorities to provide official sites for all those Travellers residing in or having recourse to their area, the level of provision to be determined by a head count. Although funding was made available from central government to develop sites, local authorities were reluctant to set up sites. By fudging the head counts - discounting Irish Travellers or counting on days when it was known large numbers would be away at family celebrations - County Councils underestimated the amount of sites they needed to provide. They were able to drag their heels because no time limit was set on responding to the Act. The county boundary changes clouded the picture even further and authorities were able to use this as a delaying tactic.

The *Caravan Act* also made it illegal for Travellers to station a caravan on land situated within the boundaries of the Highway or on occupied land. So Travellers were forced onto an insufficient number of official sites, denied recourse to stopping areas which enabled them to earn their living through travelling and made to live in conditions which went against their culture. In 1994 the *Criminal Justice and Public Order Act* repealed the *Caravan Act.* This not only relieved local authorities of responsibility to provide for Travellers but granted them greater powers of eviction. Overnight the 4,000 families - estimated to be one third of the current Traveller population - unable to secure a pitch on an unofficial site were criminalised.

The situation of the Wakefield site reflected the national state of affairs. Heath Common, known as the Jolly Sailor Site, has always been a traditional stopping place for as far back as anyone can remember. The site had already been a semi-permanent residence for members of two or three Gypsy families. The only Council provision was a standpipe for water. The lack of any other provision, toilets, electricity and rubbish collection meant the Council were falling foul of the *1968 Caravans Act.* A scheme to develop the site to bring it up to standard was thought to be too expensive so when developers BVA Park Homes approached the Council with a plan to develop the site as a private venture, the Council agreed and gave them a peppercorn rent for the first couple of years. The idea was that BVA would develop a number of transient pitches and some income generating static pitches with old holiday caravans. This was to be completed by 1989.

BVA failed to develop the site to the desired standard. Gypsy sites do not have to comply with building regulations and toilet blocks were built without foundations, wiring was faulty; the company kept no record of people using the site and so the site was overcrowded and in a desperate physical state. A Heath Common Steering Committee had been formed and held meetings attended by officers of the council, police and fire brigade and other interested parties. It lobbied to bring the problems on the site to the attention of the appropriate authorities and eventually Wakefield took over management of the site.

Expectations were high. Travellers on site were consulted about what they wanted and for a short period it looked as though things were beginning to go right. A report, *Travelling On,* was produced by Linda Richardson that outlined the historical problems with the site and ended with the upbeat sentence 'Hopefully once the council takes over responsibility, and develops it in the way families have suggested, then there will be a more settled and happier community.' But, crucially, most of the things that the Gypsies had asked for, were ignored, in particular the need for firm management, fencing around each pitch, the size of the site and the importance of living within family groupings.

This is now the situation Travellers on the Wakefield site find themselves in. They are unable to move freely around the country, earning a living as they do so. If they pull up on the roadside they are immediately moved on and there are insufficient official sites around the country to cater for a transient population. People are now afraid to leave their pitches in case it will be occupied while they are away. They are stuck on a site which, apart from being in physically poor shape, under resourced and poorly managed, does not allow them the control or autonomy necessary to live within their own traditions of extended family networks. No account has been taken of ethnic diversity - all Travellers are lumped together in one homogenous group and no distinction is made between permanent residents of the site and transient Travellers, both groups having conflicting needs and priorities.

PRIDE

born on the side of the road

My old Bedford truck is nearly forty years old, I bought it off an old fruitier who had kept it at the back of an hay barn. I keep it just for pleasure, I take it up to Appleby and Stow on the Wolds and it makes me feel good. It takes me back to my childhood, to the old times when nobody had cars, when the truck was just a working vehicle. When that truck was built I wasn't even old enough to drive, it cost £750 new, in days when you could buy a street house for £50.

They were very fashionable with Travellers when they came out. They were in fashion the same time as horse and trap and living caravans. The horse and trap didn't really go out of fashion until the mid 1960s when everyone wanted to drive and have trailers instead of living caravans. That was a big time of change for the Traveller. The motor vehicle didn't necessarily make the work easier, you might have been more comfortable if it rained, but it was just that people wanted to drive.

I was born during the war in 1942, my father was enlisted into the army. Just like everybody else, if a Traveller's name came up, the army would come and get you. If you couldn't go in the army, you worked on the farms. I think that is where a lot of the field work set off, it was good work, there was rationing on but there was always some extra vegetables and milk to be found. I have done a lot of my work in the fields. I've gathered hops, strawberries, peas, whatever there was, we had a good relationship with the farmers around Evesham and Worcester. I miss all that, the freedom of life.

Trade was different in those days. The old campfire talk, people would talk as they made pegs and flowers and little hall tables, there was a lot to be learned in that talk. Times have changed, the trade has changed. Now people who talk are talking about how much someone has got or who is smoking what, who's doing what, who's in court and who's in prison. My father was a Welshman who travelled, there are generations of us, it is different now.

I keep nine horses over in Normanton, I feed and water them twice a day. I have a Gypsy Flat Cart and a posh Governor's Cart that was built in 1910, but I only take them out in summer and on a Sunday. The traffic on the road is just too bad any other day. I love it when I have them out but these days, it's just for pleasure and a bit of pride.

Animals played a big part in the travelling life, they still do, but more so before the motor car. The horses were what pulled us from one place to the other, they were a lot slower than the motor car but it was a better life, I used to love the horses. I rode them when I was younger, but not when I was married. It is a man's job to look after the horses. If they used to see a woman riding a horse they would shout 'Look at her, she's wanting some trousers.' These days, you can't tell a man from a woman.

When we were travelling, my husband would drive the caravan and I used to drive the drey. Sometimes if it was really bad weather, then we would tie the drey to the back of the caravan. We would have eight or nine horses on the go, but only one would pull the caravan. Sometimes when we came to a steep hill, we might change the horse to get a fresh one to pull us to the top.

When we pulled onto camp my husband would take the greyhounds out coursing. We always had two or three greyhounds with us. We had one called Foxy that was so well trained, when we pulled on, it would go out by itself to find rabbits and he would bring them back and drop them at the fire for us. That was a great dog. It eventually got poisoned and died. It was a great shame.

I do love dogs, they are great company. It's different when you are not travelling, but I still have them now. My dog Bouncer won't eat raw sausages, you have to fry them for him. He also turns his nose up at sour milk. I have cats now too. Cats were never any good when you were travelling. You'd pull up and they'd be gone. You can't tie a cat up.

It wasn't just dogs and horses. We had birds and goats. We had the goats for milk - goats milk is very good for a child born with asthma or bronchitis, the goat's milk will cure it. The birds, they were mainly as children's pets. They used to lay eggs but we

would never eat them, the kids thought that Gypsy eggs were dirty. We would also have a cock. Other families would have cocks as well and when we used to pull onto camps each family would throw their cocks together and they would fight and the one that lost would be killed. We would never eat the dead cock though, we would just throw it away.

Animals made life much easier. We didn't need as much money to live. The horses and goats would graze on the land, when they had eaten all there was to graze we would move on. The dogs would live off the scraps. The only time we had to pay out was when it was snowing and we had to buy hay for the horses. With a husband and wife and six children travelling around from place to place with all the animals surrounding us, hawking pegs and lace and picking up scrap, it was a good life.

I've never been to school a day in my life, I didn't have to. My dad gave me my first horse and trap when I was fifteen, and off I went by myself getting scrap. I'm thirty-four now and I haven't been out scrapping for three years. All the cold weather and heavy lifting takes its toll, I've got rheumatoid arthritis and my back is too bad to lift. I think the arthritis is down to the long days sat on the trap in the pouring rain, I can remember it being so cold my bones ached. The bad back is due to all the awkward lifting, it's not easy picking up cast baths and washing machines and getting them up onto the trap. My dad died of a heart attack, they reckoned it was because of all the towing and writhing he did.

It was a good job to do, you were helping people out. If they didn't have anything for you then they couldn't give and that was that. It was a sort of public service. I used to call on places about once a week and I'd ride through shouting 'Scrap Iron' and sometimes people would save things for me. I went all over the Wakefield district, out to Eastmoor, the Peacock Estate, Thornes Lane, even as far out as Featherstone. I'd go as far as the horse could manage. I'd see the other lads setting off and we'd tell each other where we were going so as not to cover the same ground.

I used to set off about nine in the morning and I would be out until I had as much scrap on as the horse could pull. Sometimes I could be back home for twelve o'clock, that would be a good day. Some days I could be out until nine at night and still come back with nothing. They were bad days, especially if it was raining. Imagine being on a horse and cart for six miles in the rain. No coat can protect you from that kind of cold.

I always knew where to go to sell the scrap, wherever I was. There isn't much money in scrap now though, I think they ship it out and sell it abroad. Everything is plastics now, even the washing machines are plastic and the baths are made of porcelain. Most of the lads now make their money cutting down trees, clearing rubbish or Tarmacing. I don't know them trades though.

I still breed horses. I love horses. In all my time as a scrap man I was never tempted to get a vehicle. You don't have to tax a horse, you don't need to put petrol in it and it will never break down on you. As long as you keep it fed and shoed, it will keep going. The horse that my dad gave me was a big black nine year old called Gypsy. I kept her until she was twenty-two. I've still got horses that I bred off her, I keep them up on the common. If I breed a colt I will sell it on, if I get a mare I will keep it for breeding. It keeps me busy, going and feeding and looking after them.

I'd been with horses all my lifetime, just like my father and uncles before me. I still have family in Ireland now who have never been over here and they are still dealing in horses. But horses bust me up many years ago now and I have never worked with them since.

We would take horses from one fair to another. Usually we would have nine or ten horses at a time, some of the lads would have up to twenty. We would have bought them in Ireland, the Irish horses are always the best, and then sell them over here. Some days we could sell three or four horses in an hour, and sometimes we might go weeks without any interest.

We would travel miles to fairs, looking after the horses all the way. I can remember many times the horses would break out and my father would be sending me after them.

It might be two o'clock in the morning before I would be catching up with them and bringing them back.

I was trying to stop galloping horses when I got busted. I was painting a caravan and it was a sunny day and the kids were out playing. Some of the kids were playing with the horses and they started to run. I went out to try and stop them and that's when they hit me. My arm was pulled out, my head was kicked in, I was very nearly dead. My brothers managed to tie the horses up and save me, if it wasn't for them I wouldn't be alive now. I went to Pinderfields Hospital and spent a very long time there. When I eventually came out I said I would never work with horses again, and I never have.

My wife still had a horse. She used to go out hawking with a horse and trap. She loves horses like me, her father was a great horse man. But still I miss working with them. I wish I could be doing it now. I was just getting good with them when I was hurt. The best horse I ever saw was one I bred. It was a black and white one called Speed. She could trot anywhere, she was very fast. I had her until a right old age and then I had her knackered. She could still go then.

We don't have any horses now. We are too old anyway, but the motor wagon put an end to the horse. Some men still have some horses up on the Common, but the young men now want a good car and a lorry. It is all very sad, I really miss the horses.

My life changed on 19 August 1982. My daughter had been to a wedding in Castleford and as she was driving back over Pineapple Hill on the edge of Heath Common she had an accident. The accident happened at four o'clock in the afternoon, she died at ten o'clock that night in Pinderfields Hospital. There were four people in the car and I think they must have been messing about, Madeleine was the only one to be killed. Ever since that day, nothing has been the same. We never really cared what happened after that, it is very hard to recover.

I had ten kids, four daughters and six sons. Of the surviving ones, all of them live in houses. That is except one son Johnny, I haven't seen or heard from him in fourteen

years. He was the father of Cathlyn who lives with me now, and I have brought up like a daughter. One of my sons goes out Tarmacing and he is married to a girl from Wakefield, the rest of them are married to Travellers but don't live the Traveller life.

When you have Romany blood, you want to roam. I have got arthritis and angina so I'm stuck here now, and my husband is in the cemetery in Doncaster, next to my daughter, his mam and dad and some of my Hanrahan family are buried there. My father lived to be 101 years old and he travelled all his life. An Irishman from County West Meath, he died 27 years ago. I was on this site when I heard the news.

All of my children were born on the side of the road, and if I was to tell the truth, I would have to say that I wish that my children were still travelling. You have got to be who you are and we are Romany. But it is very hard to travel nowadays and the Gypsy are not what they used to be. I have never lived in a house a day in my life. I'm afraid to be in one. I fear that if I go up the stairs then the house might fall in on me. I go and visit my son in his house, but I will only stay a few hours. I never went to school, I can't even write my own name or tell the time. I have an idea what time it is by the light of the day, but I have to shout Cathlyn to tell it to me. The younger ones need to know these things and it makes them different.

It has been a difficult life since Madeleine died. My son wanted to buy me a new caravan, but I told him I was happy with the one I have. It's an old one and it's not in the best of condition but it is what I know, I am more used to it, it's my home.

The Gypsy shows a lot of respect to the dead. The funerals are usually big and traditional affairs. My husband died in a terrible accident, leaving me with three young children. I was living on Mexborough at the time and he was killed up at Rotherham, he was getting some scrap and he was hit by a big Hi-ab crane.

They kept my husband away until two days before the funeral, when he was brought to the caravan and laid out. Word gets out by telephone and word of mouth and people start coming, there can be two or three hundred sat around and then more will

turn up on the day. People go out and get loads of wood to keep a big fire going and there will be lots of cups of tea made. There is no eating of meat until after the funeral, you will have tomato sandwiches, but no ham.

Depending on the type of death, the widow is usually too devastated to do much, so everyone rallies around. My husband's death was a tragic shock, I wasn't in any state. My father-in-law was a great help to me at the time, but the shock to him of his son dying meant he was never the same again. Widows usually wear black for twelve months in respect to their husband. I wore black for five years because I lost my mother and grandmother around the same time.

My husband was laid out in the caravan in an open coffin so people could come and see him. He was never left on his own, somebody was always with him. White sheets covered the inside of the caravan and someone close took responsibility for lighting candles and making sure they never went out.

The horse and trap came and collected him and took him to the cemetery in Doncaster. On the same day as the burial, all the curtains in the caravan were closed. Some good Samaritan stayed behind and made sure they were all opened when we were gone. His sisters went through all his belongings, looking for sentimental things to keep, then everything else, all his possessions, were put into the caravan and the whole lot was burnt. Nobody wants a caravan if someone in it died, so you are as well off burning it, plus you can't sell anything that belonged to someone who died. I still have a pony that belonged to my husband and it costs money to feed it, but I couldn't sell it.

I was left with three children and a pram with a few clothes in it. My nerves were going wild at the time and there were no health visitors. I had to move into a house with my parents in Dunbar Street, Wakefield. Everyone did their best for me and it took six months for me to get a caravan on this site. When I came here there was about sixteen caravans and the ground was covered in red stuff. It was a cold and wet caravan. I can remember when the gas conked, we were all shaking round a candle trying to keep warm.

My husband died at Christmas time. My wish now is that I could afford to get all my Christmas presents before they start playing that music in the shops. When I hear that music, I'm reminded of all the bad memories.

My mother died when I was eleven years old. We were up on a site in Newcastle, and I was left to bring up my three sisters. I did all the cooking and cleaning and washing and going to the shops. It's not an easy thing for a young girl to do.

My mother was a good friend to me. We used to talk, and if I wanted a cigarette, she would give me one. My sisters don't remember her like I do, they were too young. Before she died, she converted to being a Christian and Jesus took away the pain, she didn't take any more morphine and Jesus gave her six more months of life. I'd never seen a dead person before I saw my mum.

It is said that Prices and Lees don't mix and that they should never marry. Mum was a Lee and Dad was a Price. My mum was pregnant eight times, but four of the babies were beaten out of her by my dad. He was a useless drunk and I hated him. I have seen him running a knife through my mum's head, he was killing her. He even tried to molest my little sister. He was a horrible man, but Gypsy girls are clean and they believe in being with only one man, so my mum had to stay with him. When she died we put all her possessions in the caravan, took it down the road, smashed the windows, poured petrol inside and set it on fire. I took my mum's name, I should have been a Price after my dad, but I hated him so much, I took my mum's name, Lee.

I took up with my husband when I was sixteen, he's a Price. He first told me how he felt about me at Appleby, saying how much he fancied me and wanted to be with me, but I told him I wasn't interested. He was very keen though and said he would come back for me. About six months later, I'd had a terrible row with the family and stormed out in a temper. He drove by me and stopped, asking if I wanted to go for a drive. We were in Manchester at the time. After a good bit of driving I realised we were going under the Dartford Tunnel. He pulled over and again told me how much he fancied me

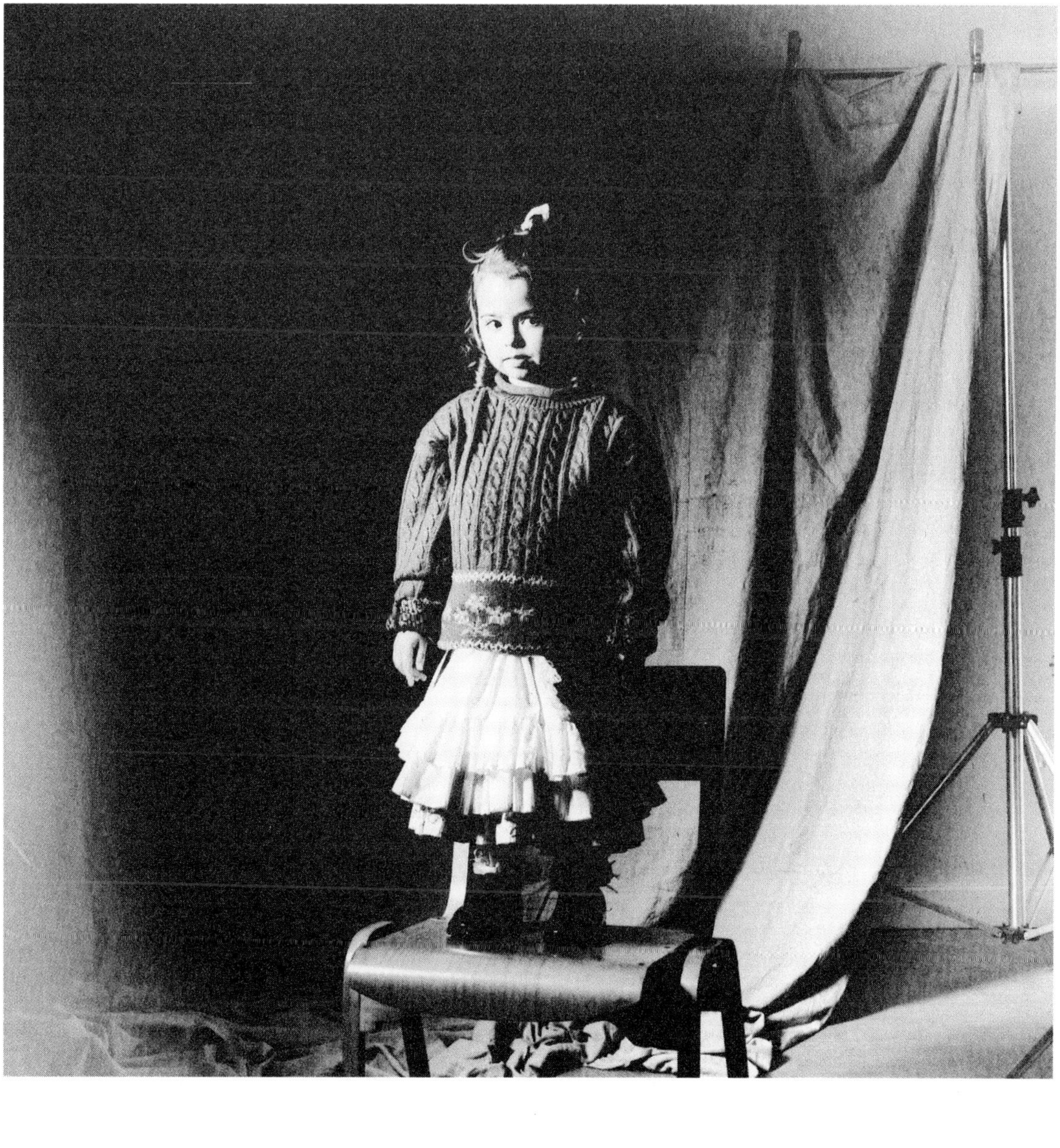

and asked me if would marry him. I told him I had no choice, I would never get back that night, so even if I did go back they would kill me. Gypsy girls are clean and only have one man, so if you spend the night out with a man, that's it, you're married. Even if nothing happened, which didn't that night, they would never believe you.

We hid out in London for a while. We didn't need to have a wedding service or anything, we were just married. I had my first child when I was seventeen, we named him Phillip after his father, though we call him Tash. I've got four children now and they are the most important things in my life. My life is for my children.

My husband's dad came from the West of Ireland but the woman he married wasn't a Traveller. His mum came from a little village called Killashandra. They travelled down in the early years.

My mother-in-law was a country girl. She had never been involved with Travellers. When she and her future husband came to the Chapel to be married, because he was a Traveller, the priest didn't want to marry them. She said 'I've come to the house of God and I intend to marry' and they were. They didn't have anywhere to live so she stayed with her mother while he went off to work and got the price of a cover and then they went. They were travelling for ten years and when she came back her family didn't recognise her.

Her husband became a soldier. He was first in the Irish army and lost one eye and then he joined the English because they would take anyone. They'd take you if you only had one leg. So he volunteered and was away in the war for three years and eleven months. She said, 'If he comes home alive I'll drink and smoke'. So when he did, she had a sip of beer and two puffs on a fag and was sick for four days. They had eleven children. He was a tinsmith and used to make and mend buckets. He was also a great painter with the trailers. He was very good to his children with their aches and pains and had his own cures for different things. If they had convulsions he would put them upside down and put two drops of brandy on the top of their mouths.

I first met my husband when I was thirteen at Appleby Fair and we met up every year until I was 16. I had lots of boys as friends but he was my only boyfriend. We wanted to get married but my Dad wanted us to wait until we were older but we wanted to marry then so we ran away for two days. We didn't sleep together or anything because I wouldn't do that before I was married. But then they had to let us get married. It's very strong with us that a woman has only one man. People think that Gypsies just move in together and have children but then what would happen if he left you after a few years and went off with another woman. Then your children would be bastards. So we got married in the registry office here. My sister did the same thing. She married my husband's brother. I took her to a convention in Wales and she ran away with him. I had to tell my parents. They thought it was a planned job but it just happened.

There is this little thing called shame between men and women that grows big with Gypsies. They're extra strict with the girls. If a girl falls pregnant she never lives it down. All her life, she will be talked about. Men are different. Men are in charge, they're the breadwinners, they make the rules. There's been a big change in our culture already. It may not look like it when you're on site but the fact that the men let gaujes come on site at all, that they can come into caravans is a big change. But there is still a separation. Girls spend time with their mothers, boys with their fathers. Women keep women's things to themselves. We don't talk about pregnancy or periods with men, it just wouldn't happen. Men want to keep the cultures separate but they marry out more than the women do. They can sleep with anyone, with gaujes, it doesn't bring shame to them. In our church it's only the men who can get up and teach and preach. We can make tea, clean, talk to other women and help them with things she can't tell a man. The women hold meetings in our trailers and the men go to Bible study in Doncaster.

In our home it was my father decided everything, made every decision, even down to what bottles the baby would have or what kind of cot. My mother just went along with it. So I always thought it was the man who made the decisions. But when I married,

it didn't happen. He would sit there saying nothing and I would be waiting for him to say something and the children were doing what they liked. And I waited and waited for him to do or say something. Then one day it clicked that he was never going to, he was the silent partner. I didn't want to take that bit on. I wanted to be close to my children, to love them, not be the one telling them off. Most wives do what their husbands tell them but I make up my own mind. I'll always apologise if I know I've been in the wrong but I won't give in when I know I'm right.

It was that way with Adam and Eve, God made Adam first and then he made Eve as a companion.

Everyone depends on me. I've got three caravans to clean out, mine, my mum's and my brother's. My mum's a fit healthy woman but since I've come here I do everything.

When you clean the caravans you take all the bunks out and all the cupboards. The carpets are all washable. The pots are taken outside and hosed down. We spend a lot on bleach and disinfectant - you have to with the dogs. We use different bowls for washing our clothes, our pots, ourselves. Right from being little I would stand on a crate to wash the windows. You weren't made to, you just did. Now when my niece comes in she'll ask, 'What can I do, what can I clean?'

The Gypsy eats different to the gauje, especially when we are travelling. I remember when I was pregnant I craved hedgehog. I used to be sending my husband out looking for them. I bet you don't get many gauje women doing that. I loves hedgehog, especially in a sandwich with plenty of salt on or in a stew. You get the hedgehog and throw him on the fire, then watch him as he swells up into a big black ball and all his spikes fall off. Then you take him off, slit him down the middle and take all his guts out and then throw him in the pot.

We eat a lot better when we are travelling. When you are stuck in one place you go to the same butcher and same shop and things taste the same, whereas when you travel

you'll be trying different butchers. And food tastes better when you can cook outside with the big black pots on an open fire. I like to make broths, all kinds of broths, rabbit broth, pheasant broth, whatever we've got. I'll put the swede in first, then the carrots, cabbage and potatoes and butter and then serve. Lots of butter, we like greasy food.

When we are travelling we will call in on abattoirs and get sheep panch, which is the sheep's piss bag and a bit like tripe. No one else wants it so we can get it cheap, for one or two pound you can feed ten families. It's a smelly meat, so you wash it and then boil it and boil it. Then you can fry it for your breakfast. You can get pig panch as well, but I wouldn't eat that if you gave me a thousand pound.

On this site we get in trouble if we light fires so we cook inside. But we still eat a lot. We eat when we are hungry, sometimes seven or eight meals a day. And when we have tea or coffee, we will eat biscuits and toast, sometimes eight slices of toast.

Food plays a big part in the celebrations for Christmas. I will get a turkey, four ducks, a big goose, roast ham, boiled ham, pork and all the vegetables. We will go through six and seven tins of Quality Street, and loads of bottles of pop. And my husband eats more than any gauje. He eats all day. The other night he ate six lamb chops and then a pack of chocolate biscuits with a cup of tea all to himself.

As soon as you are born, your earrings are put in. If you are born in a hospital these days, they don't like you piercing the baby's ear, but as soon as they come home, they are done. Everyone has their own jobs, and for my children, it was my aunt who put their earrings in.

The best kind of earring is the dollar, they are antiques now and are handed down. I still have the earrings passed on to me from my grandmother when I was four years old. If my daughter has a daughter of her own, I will pass them down to her. There are two kinds of dollar, the American and the Indian. The Indian one is bigger. The ones that I have are over a hundred years old, they are antiques. You can't get them now, you can get restrikes, as some mothers get for their daughters, but they're not proper ones.

The young ones now wear a lot of jewellery, but it is mainly the kind you can buy in the shops, there is no point in handing them down when you can just go out and buy some more. For the men, they like a good buckle on their harness. They have buckles shaped like horse shoes.

I learnt a lot about living from my grandmother. I used to go fortune telling with her, from door to door. I remember once going out with her and I was wearing a new coat. One woman was very rude to us and slammed the door in our face and my coat was caught in the door so we couldn't leave. My grandma was knocking on the door for the woman to free the coat but she wouldn't open that door for nothing, so in the end we had to get a pair of scissors and cut off the piece of coat that was stuck. I will never forget that.

I have heard stories that before my time, my grandma would pull up on a site, grab a chicken, ring it's neck and that would be tea for the night. I don't remember that but I do remember the greyhounds and lurchers catching the rabbits. They were taught to hunt, kill and carry. Some got so good at it that they would do it all by themselves. My grandma had a cat called Phoebe that could do it.

Most of our life was taken up by what was around us. My grandma used to know where to find snails in the cracks in the walls that the farmers had made themselves. They were called bowreys and you used to boil them. They were a luxury, a bit like prawns now. Us children used to catch fish with just our hands, we called it tidling. We also used to suck eggs that we found in birds' nests.

For hawking, my grandma showed us how to make pegs from Elder wood, and the flowers that we hawked were Elder as well. For the lace, everybody would chuck some money in and somebody would go off to Nottingham and get enough for all. I don't go hawking or telling fortunes now because I'm a Christian and I see it as a bad thing, but I still have my grandma's crystal ball that she passed on to me. As a Christian I should really throw it away, but I haven't got it in my heart to do it.

When she was getting older, my grandma worried all the time about dying in bad

weather. She wanted to be buried up on Appleby Hill, but if the weather was really bad she wouldn't have been able to get there. She worried for years. In the end she died in July in beautiful weather and we carried out her wish and buried her up on Appleby Hill where a lot of the Nicholsons are buried.

My grandad was Jimmy Berry, the caravan maker. He was born in June up on Appleby Hill, he is buried on Appleby Hill, and every year at the Appleby Fair, you still see his name on the back of caravans that he made.

Jimmy Berry was the best caravan maker in the country, and people knew it. The caravan that is in York Museum was made by him. He also made a lot for a Tom Thumb place in Stratford, there are all sorts of traps, fireman's ones, milkman's, butcher's, everything. He didn't just make caravans, he fixed them as well. If people wanted work doing, they used to track him down. It was like ASDA, if something is good in ASDA then word will get out and people will go, that is how it was with my grandad. If people wanted their caravan fixing, word would get out to see Jimmy Berry and they would find him. I can remember him making brushes out of his hair. Not the big painting brushes, just little thin lining ones.

He was famous in his day. He was once on that TV show *What's My Line*. He came on and where they sign their name in, he just did a scrawl. The panel didn't guess what he did, so he won. His nephew wrote a song about him which we have still got on tape.

My grandad was Chase Price, a famous bare knuckle prize fighter. If you go into some pubs in Wales, they still have photos of him on the wall. He was killed by his wife. They got into an argument and she hit him in the throat with a flat-iron. It caused him to have a blood clot that burst and it choked him to death. Today, surgeons would have been able to save him, but he just died. He is buried in Cowbridge.

My son is Chase, named after him. I'm teaching him the old Romany language and the ways of life. The language seems to be getting lost somewhere down the line. On

sites like this, the culture is disappearing. I will pass it on to my son, I'd like him to have his own lorry and go out and be able to look after himself.

Things should be passed on through the family. Each family has it's own ways. The Price family has it's own way. You can meet up with a Price anywhere, and even if you have never seen them before, you will get on with them if you are a Price. It's just a way of life. I can't travel any more and that is something I really miss, travelling is the good life. It's very difficult to travel these days and a lot is going to be lost.

We went off travelling for five months this summer and it has done me the world of good. I'm a lot brighter now, I feel different. I've never lived in a house a day in my life, but before this trip we were thinking about it. There has been a lot of trouble on this site and guns have been going off and I felt uncomfortable. When we set off on the trip, we didn't even know if we were coming back.

We spent a week here, a week there, sometimes we were only allowed twenty-four hours in places. We went to the Mission in Barnsley and then on to Appleby. We only spent three days in Appleby. I don't enjoy Appleby as much as I used to. My father died when I was there two years ago, so it reminds me of that, and now I'm a Christian I don't drink and I've never seen any sense in going to discos and acting silly. I don't go near pubs either, when Jesus comes back he won't come back in a pub.

We then pulled into the convention at Birmingham. We found a nice spot with all the family and met lots of nice people. We would spend the mornings in prayer meetings, have meetings throughout the day and sing at night. It is a really happy time. We then came back up to Castleford where there are some people and then we moved around the Wakefield area before settling back on the site for the winter and to put my son in school. I'm just hoping we go off again next summer.

I do a lot of looking after. I give my life to my nieces and nephews, my mum and my family. I have a life of being clean. Even from when I was seven or eight I would be

sitting on the floor cleaning the cups or polishing. That's what I'll do in my life. I'll marry a travelling man who will provide, and I'll stay here and clean and shop for my mam. I don't go out to work. I used to go telling fortunes but I don't any more. It's the work of the Devil. There's nothing mysterious or magical about it. Just being canny and crafty; picking things up, finding out what it was you wanted to hear. Gypsies can talk their way round things and they thought they could talk their way into heaven.

I was born in a Bill Wright waggon at Scotch corner in January, with the snow as tall as the telegraph poles. My mother carried me miles through snow and ice to get me christened. I was christened C of E. When we were young my mammy would say you couldn't do anything wrong because God was watching you so I believed in God. My children were brought up in the Roman Catholic faith - my husband was a Catholic. We did the usual things, not eat meat on a Friday, that sort of thing, but it was more a social religion.

Looking back on my childhood I wonder however did our mothers cope? There were twelve of us in our family, eight boys and four girls. The boys used to sleep in another accommodation, which might be a tent or a sheet pulled over the shafts. My mother would make a bit of bread in the morning, even when it was pouring or water cakes which was just water and flour. We never ever got took to a doctor. My mother would rub creams in and she used to make remedies for the horses. There were no fridges and we had home cured bacon and butter stored between docken leaves. Farmers were happy to sell us things and I'd be sent out to get two pennorth of milk but some of it would be drunk by the time I got back. I must have been about five after the war when things were still being rationed. We were outside Berwick when I went up to a house and asked the lady for some tea. I was expecting some in a twist of paper but she gave me two half pound packets. Well my name was up!

Years ago we could stop where we wanted on the roadside or down an old lane. We were safer then and we would wait there while our mum was out shopping. We travelled more in the horse and waggons than we do now in the motors. We had to, to find fresh

grass for the horses and the chumps out of the hedges for the fires. We would make a stake fire outside and feed every child from it. Everyone looked after everyone's children. If you came back with a few sweets they'd be given out to those children around. We didn't know what new clothes meant but wore what was begged or picked from the rags at market. With there being so little room we didn't have spare clothes - there was nowhere to store them. There might be a new dress for Appleby - like the second week in June a new satin frock was put on us. But when you begged you collected for everyone. If a pair of shoes didn't fit you they might fit someone else and that way all the children were clothed. Nowadays things are bought new all the time and you only buy for your own.

We were well cared for but we were frightened of people. If a strange lady came she might be from the school board and we were hidden away. When we were travelling we were hidden down below, under the boards. We were scared the children would be taken away. My father was fifty-three when he died and my mother wouldn't go to get the pension. She had two or three grown up sons and she was scared they'd be taken off her. It was a sheltered life.

I worked with my mother since I was nine years old. The girls did most of the work. We used to sell lace from Nottingham and a few flowers. We'd make wooden flowers out of Elder and take bark from the trees and put scent on and sell them. I also used to read fortunes. That was how I used to make my living. But now I'm born again I don't do any fortune telling. It's the work of the Devil.

We were in New Biggin, by the sea, stood on a roadside by a little wood. I must have been nine or ten. We had a crystal wireless and my mum used to listen to Billy Graham on Radio Luxembourg, late at night - 12 o'clock. We used to wonder at how he managed to keep on talking, never stopping. That was about fifty years ago. He was a young man then. But it didn't have any effect on me.

Then eight years ago I was in Chester Le Street, County Durham. I was on a Gypsy caravan site and these people - a pastor and his wife - came from Manchester. I'd seen

the pastor's lady before so she was familiar. She worked in the Supermarket on the meat counter and we used to crack jokes. Now people had come to me for years to talk about religion. I gave them a cup of tea and a biscuit and told them I knew God, smoking like a chimney all the time but you see it didn't mean anything. My time hadn't come yet. The pastor and his wife had this meeting in one of the caravans. There were thirteen or fourteen of us, all sat up and down on the seats and on the floor. And when people were praying, saying their own words, I was just saying the *Our Father*. But I felt my heart pushed up and tears pushed out. But it wasn't a sad crying. I didn't know what was happening so I asked the pastor's wife to come to my caravan. She told me that it was the Holy Spirit, that I'd been touched by the Holy Spirit. It took that little spark to set me off.

PREJUDICE *looking over your shoulder*

My daddy was the old kind of Traveller, a lovely man. He wouldn't have no mess or boys blaggarding. Things were kept clean and decent. He was a scrap dealer and would clean people's yards in exchange for a bit of scrap. He was known by the council men all round Leeds and Bradford. They knew him so well they'd give us loads of time to go when we had to move off and sometimes they wouldn't even bring him the eviction papers because they knew if they said we had to be off by the Saturday we'd gone by the Friday night. But in spite of that we're still tormented. We've been fired at with shotguns, with air-rifles and petrol bombed.

Ten years ago we were down in Tamworth. We were only three caravans, our family in one, my mam and dad in another and my sister and brother-in-law in another. We'd pulled onto a bit of grass for the night and when we woke up in the morning there was a petrol bomb at the end of the trailer, soaked but it hadn't caught. It was only a small trailer and if it had gone up there would be no way for us and our two babies to get out.

Seven years ago we were down at the end of a lane. It was in the middle of winter and freezing cold. Late at night we heard a car revving up outside the trailer. Joe, my husband, went to the door to see what was happening but I said 'For God's sake don't go out'. I thought it might be the police and if you step out they can take you off and be questioning you for hours. He had his hand on the door but had just turned back inside when they shot at the caravan and tore the top of the roof off with a double barrelled shotgun. When we looked in the morning there were cartridges where they had fired from. We reported it to the police but they weren't very helpful.

We don't like to be together in small groups. It's not safe. We get harassed from residents and from the police. They see all Travellers as being the same, they lump us together as trouble makers. When there are only a few of you, you can't defend yourself.

There was almost a riot down in Stoke-on-Trent. There were only four trailers, just our family, and we pulled on. Almost immediately a crowd of about 50 people came down with stones and bottles and one man waving a long knife, as broad as your hand. But the police didn't stop him, or the crowd. They said there had been trouble with another group and they'd have to move us for our own safety. No-one had told us there had been trouble with a group of Travellers there before us. They thought we would just know about it because everyone thinks Travellers are all like each other and know everything about all the rest. My mam said it was always the quiet ones who will pay for it.

We'd come down to York to buy this new trailer and were travelling back to Windsor. Tommy was with us and his trailer broke down. So we pulled onto the car park of a small railway station. It was not a good place because it was surrounded by trees and wasn't safe, you couldn't see around you. This was about nine o'clock. The police came up and we explained we were only staying the night, stopping until the men could fix the trailer and they said OK. The men went off to fix the trailer. Then there must have been a change of shift because a new lot of police came down. They were effing and blinding, the language coming out was nobody's business, telling us we had to go straight away. They said they'd be bringing in a vehicle to tow us off. We told them the men weren't there, that they'd gone to fix the trailer but they didn't believe us and were shouting at the men to come out of hiding. One of the women went and got her husband but when he tried to drive back onto the car park they refused to let him on. They couldn't get us off but they turned the sirens on and stayed there all the night. It was dreadful.

We moved into a place in Gloucester, in the Cattle Market. The police came and told us to move, but before we could do anything about it, they were picking stuff up from outside, rubbish and dog muck and just threw it into the caravans. My father-in-law got a bit funny about it and got arrested. Then when they arrested him his wife panicked and started shouting at them. She was terrified of the police and was taken down to the

EDFO D
JUST DO IT.
MN 5819

station and kept there for five hours. She had to give her brother-in-law's address because a trailer isn't seen to be a home, so that they could release her to a proper address.

You can't just pull up any longer. When you pull up onto a piece of land the landowner comes down and marks out the piece of land that you're on, colours that in on the map. He goes to court and swears an affidavit and he can say anything on that affidavit. Then you have to be off in seven days and if you don't they compound your vans and vehicles. But we never wait that long. We're off straight away.

On the night of the trouble, there was shooting and the police were called. There were police helicopters going backwards and forwards over the site and the police were up at the top, shouting over the loudspeakers and telling everyone to come out of the caravans with their hands up; children, babies, everyone. We had to walk up to the man in the office and he identified all those he knew. Some people had friends and relatives staying with them but he couldn't identify them and they got arrested. I was expecting John, and Ellie May was just a small baby. I had to lift her out of her chair because they were looking for guns. Those people who had locked their caravans got their doors kicked in by the police when they were going round searching.

We were all put in the pub. We're not the kind of people who go into pubs, we're born again Christians. People were smoking and the smoke was killing my baby's lungs. My mother was living in a house so I asked to leave and go up there. It was good that the police were called but we were treated like dogs, all of us were treated like criminals. After that night a lot of people just pulled off the site. People who had lived here for years, left. The Prices had been here for eighteen years and they went to Selby and never came back. They were pensioners and were too old to just be able to travel for a while and then come back. Travelling is hard. You only have the trailer heated for a few hours a day, you don't have water on tap and you have to pull up on the roadside and then there's all the problems with that. They didn't want the trouble with that or the trouble here.

I remember once I'd gone into a chemist to get some face cream and Tash, my son, was crying for mouthwash, so I got him some and he put it in his pocket. In the next shop I was in, I could see that they were watching me, like they always do. I got my shopping and went to the check-out and paid for the lot and they came up to me saying I'd been stealing. I'd told them I'd paid for everything and they said that I hadn't paid for what was in the boy's pocket. I was mad. They shouldn't be making accusations like that, I showed them the receipt and I can remember throwing some bananas at this woman. She ended up holing herself in a cupboard. But it was their fault, they were only making accusations because I am a Gypsy.

Tash has been accused of taking shoes off people's feet. It's ridiculous, he has plenty of shoes. I don't wear shoes, so people say things. When I pick up my kids from school, they say things to my kids. The kids have asked me to wear shoes now when I pick them up, so I don't draw attention to them. What I do is put a pair of shoes in the pram and when I get close to the school I put them on just to stop people from talking. You should see the shopkeepers watch me when I'm walking round their shop with no shoes on my feet.

We can get our clothes back from the launderette and we will find our clothes are all mixed up. I once got some pregnant clothes in my washing that belonged to Gilly and she had some of mine. The launderette woman just sees us as Gypsies and puts all our clothes in together. They don't care. It is very difficult when we are travelling to get a launderette. You will see signs saying 'No Travellers' and all you want to do is get some clean blankets. You get fed up. Prejudice is worst when you really need something.

The way we're treated in shops, it gets me so angry I want to take them to court. I know some people do go down to the Ridings and rob, but I have never stolen in my life. They don't see me as a separate person, they see me as a Gypsy, but my leg isn't joined to someone else's and my arm's my own. I am separate but we all get classed the same. If I go into *Bangles and Bows* in the Ridings and I might be looking for a hair

bobble, one of the shop-girls will come and stand behind me and another one will pretend to fix a tray of earrings just down by the side of me. They think we're too thick to notice what's going on. Then you begin to feel like it's a challenge and you want to take something just to fix them. Before I was a Christian I used to get abusive. I used to say to the girls in the shops; 'Look at you. You're dossers - working for £20 a week'. They'd think I was a nobody with nothing, but I probably had more in my pocket than they would earn that week. I don't do that now. But they're really nasty to us.

My mum went there looking for a slide, not knowing that we had had all this trouble with them, it was for a wedding or some do. She wanted a beige one and they didn't have one so she asked the girl if there was a shop nearby that sold them. The girl said to try the shop next door. She went next door but it was selling mobile phones. When she went back to *Bangles and Bows* to confront the girl who had sent her they said she was hiding in the back and she wouldn't come out.

It was my daughter's birthday and I went in to collect a cake I'd had made for her. My son came in saying a man had punched him in the face. I was in a temper and I went down in the car and confronted him.

'You hit a child yesterday.' He didn't deny it.

'Yes, I did. One of them was giving me cheek. There were two kids on their bikes.'

I asked him which one it was, asked him to give a description. He told me that it was the one on the front bike but he couldn't reach him so he'd hit the dark haired one, my son, at the back. Can you believe it? Now I know young boys in a crowd do get up to things but my boys never give cheek or swear. I was in such a temper I threatened him, telling him I would burn his shop down to the ground. I told him our men had come looking for him. And if the welfare came round asking why my son had got bruises on his face I'd send them to him. He said he was sorry and that I should send the men round and he'd apologise to them. But that wouldn't be a good idea.

'One day' I said, 'you'll be on your own. Keep looking over your shoulder.'

At the weekend two or three motors will go from the site to *Bootleggers*, a Gypsy disco in Newark. Young Gypsy people come from all over the country, usually there are two to three hundred people there, but at busy times like Christmas, it might be too busy to get in. I used to go to *Roof Top Gardens* in Wakefield but there was usually trouble. The gauje men would think that the Gypsy girls have a dirty reputation and they make moves on you and then when a Gypsy boy comes over and warns them off there will be a big fight and the Gypsy will be thrown out. Once one Gypsy is banned, all Gypsies are banned.

It is very difficult to mix. The only time I will mix with a gauje is in a shop when they are serving me, and then I am under suspicion of stealing and they watch me all the time I am in. Shoplifters love to see Gypsies out shopping, they know that the security guard will take their eyes off them for a while. Shops can put up signs that say 'No Travellers', that is discrimination, they can't do that to anybody else.

At school I was an outsider, I hated it. I went to Sandal Magna and got good reports, but I just couldn't mix. It is only the Gypsy man that has respect for a Gypsy woman. When we are travelling, with grass under our feet not concrete, the young people make an effort to get together. Word will be put out that there is a party and everyone will make the effort. When Appleby is on, we will go to a disco in Carlisle. I know people from all over the country, not just one school. We have our own ways and so we get on better with each other.

I can mix with anyone and that's because I lived in houses and went to school. A lot of people can only mix with their own kind, mostly people who haven't been to school. You learned to mix there. Reading and writing's got a lot to do with it. There's an embarrassment about mixing with people they don't know if they can't read and if they don't understand the words people use. I taught myself to read. I was only at school for three weeks and it was heaven. You know how on the first day you can be terrified, well I wasn't because the headmaster made me welcome, the teachers made me welcome.

Life at home was hell so school was a real break. I was three weeks off being ten and I remember that because on my tenth birthday we were off again and I never went back.

Most Gypsies threaten children with school. They hold it out as a punishment 'You carry on like that and you're going to school tomorrow' I've heard that one over and over from my dad. We were terrified when he said school. Then when I went it was heaven, I couldn't wait for the next day to come. So I tried to pass this onto my children. They're going to learn, not to be ignorant of the world. They're going to see both ways of life, not just the Gypsy's. My daughter's at school. My husband wants her to leave. She's learnt to read and write and use computers and now he wants her to learn our way of life. He wants her to learn to clean and to look after children. She gets on at school and mixes with gaujes and then our girls don't mix with her. They say she's a gauje. I want her to stay at school. I want her to have a different way of life from cooking and bringing up children. It's important to learn about the world outside the caravan site. I want my daughter to learn our way of life. She's learnt to read and write and use computers and is she going to give that up to learn to clean and bring up children? But I have to fight for her to stay on. He says I've had my way now it's her turn to learn the Gypsy way of life. But it's important for her to learn the world outside the Gypsy site, not to stay in the old way of life.

When family allowance first came out I was up on the Honeypot site in Darlington. I went down to the Post Office to collect my money and the man there was shouting at me 'You've got to write your name.' I couldn't write it, I'd never been to school a day in my life. The man was really angry, he couldn't understand. When I went in again he was still angry but after a few weeks he started to realise what the problem was and he learnt me how to do my signature so I can do that now.

I never went to school because I didn't need to. You don't when you are travelling. But now, because it is difficult to travel and life is getting faster, you need to read more. If I need to catch a bus I will be there flagging every bus down just to ask the driver if

he is going where I want to go. Sometimes if the driver is in a bad mood because he has had a hard day, he will be shouting and cursing at me and I feel like an animal. They look at me as though I'm not right and that it is me to blame.

I have lived my life by learning to recognise things. I know what is beans and what is coffee, not because what it says on the label, just that it looks like a tin of beans and a jar of coffee. If you buy some foods you have to ask people how long it takes to cook them. I can't even take any of the free samples and tastes they have in supermarkets. If I see the stand, I have to walk past pretending I am in a hurry because they always ask you to sign for this and that or fill in your details or write down what you think of things. I know prices of things and I know my ABCs. I know the letters, I just can't make them into words. I had a telephone for two and half years and didn't know the number.

I would like to learn to read now but I think I am too old. It would be nice to read the Bible. About ten years ago when I was on at Doncaster, it was arranged for some of us to go to night school to learn to read and write. I went for six months. The teacher was called Paula and she was really nice, we learnt numbers and such, but they put us in with people who couldn't learn, people with special needs. They needed special care, they needed love and attention. They had hats with badges all over them, three or four hundred badges. They would ask us if we wanted a cup of tea and within two minutes there would be tea-bags flying all over the place, in the air. It would be a disaster. We would end up making the tea for them. We spent most of our time looking after them. I left after six months. We just couldn't learn anything with them.

I wanted my children to learn to read, it is so important these days. My daughter can help me out with some reading and the men in the office will tell me how much my electricity bill is and will read any letters I get. It is too late now for me to learn.

Looking back, I don't want what I had for myself for my daughter, Frances. I want Frances to be something. I want her to go to school and to learn to read and write. I

want my daughter to be whatever she wants to be and my husband thinks that way as well. I never got that choice. My mother was a good scholar. She was going to join the army but gave it up when she was married. Me daddy came from Limerick. He was reared in Limerick the hard way and he wasn't keen on anything. It didn't matter to him if I went to school or not. I went to a school in Ireland for travelling children and made my Holy Communion but there were twelve children younger than me and I had to be at home to look after them. All the mistakes I will correct for Frances. I don't care what other people here think about her going to school or if she wants to work. You have to go your own way. My sister-in-law is married to a Pakistani and has four children with him. That was scandalous in our culture but she did it and I know from her you can do whatever you set your mind to. Her children were brought up in their father's way. They went to school and one is a foreman, another one is a garage mechanic. She visits the family and she's accepted by the family but not by other Travellers.

I'd pay money to be off this site but my son is settled at school and it's the first school he's liked. He went to one when he was six. I was just passing one day and I decided to look in. He was standing there in the playground with all the other children standing around taunting him, calling him 'Gypo - Gypo'. There was a teacher standing there, or an assistant, anyway she was supposed to be in charge and she was doing nothing. So I just took him by the hand and took him off, away from the school. The teachers must have told the children because he would never have told them himself. At this school no-one knows. He asked me if I had told the teachers and I said 'Of course, they have to know.' But they've not told the children.

I went to a special Travellers school until I was about ten, in Limerick in Ireland. It was an art school and I did sketches and embroidery. I loved it. We were taught by nuns and they could be cruel. Twice a year they would bring us on weekend trips. We were walking along and I jumped over a wall, the height of a bench, to walk to the beach.

The nun shouted at me to get off the beach and I shouted back 'I will not'. She hit me so hard I could feel the imprints of her fingers along my cheek. I had the ruler more times than I can remember, for small things like dropping pens in class.

We were living on the site when I was a little girl. My mam wanted us to go to school and she would walk us off the site every day. It was sludge and mud so we would wear Wellingtons and then when we got to the pub she changed us into our shoes and white socks. We were the only Gypsy children at Sandal Magna. I learnt to read quickly but my two sisters were slow at learning and my mam made sure they went to a school where they would get special help, so I was the only Gypsy child at Manygates Middle and then at Kettlethorpe. I wasn't bullied at school. I was with the other children from the time I was four years old, so they knew me and they knew what I was. Also, I wouldn't let anyone call me names. I knew how to look after myself. I didn't go to school to learn for a job. I knew I was going to come back to the Traveller's way of life.

I met my husband in High Wykeham. I was seventeen then and he was my first proper boyfriend. I wanted to get married but my mother wouldn't give consent. She didn't like him so I ran away. We went to my cousin in Hackney, we got our own trailer and when I was eighteen, we married in a Catholic Church. My mother never came round.

We move around all the time; we were never on a site before this but now I'm staying because the children have asthma and I want them to go to school. I want them to learn to read. I went to school in Swansea. They had a special class for children who had special circumstances - had been in hospital and the like. I also went to school in Ireland where they had special classes for Traveller children. There was this little red-haired school teacher - Miss Simmonds. She was wonderful and brought me to see a priest for my Holy Communion. My husband can't read and if I'm reading a magazine he gets frustrated and I get tormented with his questions about what is this or that. I don't want my children to be frustrated like that.

I prefer being at school but my mother needs me to be here. My mum wanted to go to school but her dad wouldn't let her. He was in and out of hospital and dads are not so bothered about that sort of thing. But she did things for herself, she was only at school for three weeks but she taught herself to read. She's been ill, she had an operation on her throat and now she's on pills that keep her alive. She needs help now because everyone puts on her. Everyone round here knows my mother and she's never down when she's off the site but everyone needs help sometimes and it's my turn to help her.

I'm like my mum, people come to me to sort things out. I like mixing with people. Wherever we moved to my mother would book us into the nearest school, Swatham, Plymouth, St Johns, Rochdale; so we were always meeting new children. I can read and write and I've been teaching others how to spell their names and to count. Classes are the best thing and I got a Head Teacher's commendation last year. I'd love to be a lawyer. I'd have to go to University. I can only go to school odd days now because I want to help my mother. But Mrs Todd from the Education Service is going to bring me work to do here so I don't fall behind. I can work in the shed or in my brother's trailer and that way I'll keep up.

Most Traveller girls finish school at thirteen or fourteen. I know one girl here who stayed all the way to sixteen but you are expected to be at home after thirteen and to help out with the cleaning and the other children. People don't mind us going to school to learn to read and write but then we have to learn the Traveller's way. Other kids on the site call us 'school girls'. Then when you are at school sometimes people at school don't see us for who we are, just that we're Gypsies. It means I'm good at arguing and standing up for myself.

When I was little I was scared of people and let them push me about. I was too soft. Once when I was staying with my Gran my cousins were going to kickboxing lessons and they taught me how. It's not good to act hard because then you get picked on, but sometimes you have to fight back and one day I kickboxed a girl and after that she left me alone. I'm alright now because I know I can defend myself.

I can't remember a lot about school, though I kind of liked it. I went to two or three schools in County Durham but I was never at one school for more than a month. I was never there long enough to learn to read, I sort of taught myself what I know. My brother hated it, we were taught by nuns and he used to kick their legs black and blue.

I've never heard of a Gypsy girl going to college. Say now, like me, I can read. I went to school to learn my Holy Communion and confirmation. I can read enough to fill in forms and read the Bible. No Gypsy goes to school after the age of thirteen or fourteen. Perhaps one in ten might. They don't need to. After that they're too big to be at school and they should be helping at home They're not going to get work in a factory or a shop. They wouldn't want it and they don't get trusted there. It works both ways.

We want to keep our culture, our way of life. Some of us just can't live another way of life. We've not chosen it, it's not a question of keeping this way of life instead of another way, it's just how life is. There are things that I would want to be different, but not our way of life. When I look out of my window now, right from the bottom of the site, all the way up one side and to the top are my family, my uncles and aunts and cousins. On my stand now is my brother's trailer. He travels still but he pulls up here every now and again. He used to have a stand but they wanted him to come back early, in August, and he wasn't ready to stop travelling then so he gave it up.

PLACE *off the tip*

I have been on this site longer than anyone here. When I first pulled on there was only me, Granny Nicholson and Michael Kesch, that was sometime in the 1960s. In them days it was a rough site, it had just one man's toilet, one woman's and it cost about eight shillings a week. We settled on for a long time, my husband had got sugar diabetes behind his eyes and he couldn't look, so we had to stop travelling around.

We always liked it round here. When we were first married in 1956 this area was the first we came to. We pulled onto Heath Common and Sharlston. My husband used to tell a story about Heath Common and some travellers from long ago, he told it hundreds of times. The traveller was called Smith, a proper travelling man, and he was out on the Common digging for rabbits when he found some ancient gold sovereigns in a copper kettle. His dad told him that he should take them into the police, which he did and they got a reward. The old travellers were very honest, and I think my husband liked to tell that story because he himself was an honest man, he was never in trouble with the police a day in his life.

My husband also saw the ghost that haunts these grounds. The White Lady. I know of three people who have seen her, I never want to see her as long as I'm on here.

Twenty-one years ago this place was rough. It was a waste ground. There was Nan, ourselves, the Prices and the Nicholsons and Reine Cash, all English Travellers. There weren't many people and we all knew one another. It was that rough that no-one else wanted to live on here, so we had the place to ourselves. People might pull on for a couple of days but they didn't stay. When we went up to town, to discos, we'd say we were off Doncaster or Bradford. If you said you'd come off Wakefield they said you were just come off the tip. There was a big hump in the middle which later, the council dug away. There was no bridge so when the river flooded we had to walk off the site

through the power station. When Derek was here, the first man who did up the site, he built a tin bridge over it and then when the council took it on they built a proper bridge.

The first people to do up the site didn't work for the Council, they were doing it private although the Council men used to walk round and keep an eye on things. Derek was doing the site up. He moved thirty statics on one side of the site. There were statics on one side and trailers on the other. The statics had toilets and showers in them and people out of houses came and lived in them. But they kept themselves to themselves and we didn't mix. The travellers had a tap at the end of the gate and a small square shed with a toilet and shower in it, not even big enough for a bath. There were no stands, just a concrete base for the trailers to stand on and shale around the base. There was no electricity so we had portable televisions that ran off batteries. We'd have all the lights off to keep the telly going. It cost us £3 a week to get the batteries charged. We would charge them up off the pick-up, and then push the pick-up down the hill to recharge it.

There were eight of us and the site was full of my family. Aunt Kitty lived in her massive green tent with fifteen children. This was like her kitchen tent, they had a trailer as well. She had an open fire in the middle and a Queen Anne stove. She baked bread every day and it was beautiful, the touch of real Traveller's hands. You couldn't buy anything like it in the shops. She made pegs and told fortunes and sold lucky charms. Her husband worked, looking for scrap. They were a big Catholic family, prayers were said morning and night. When I was going to bed my Mum would chuck holy water in my face and if we'd been lying it would sting.

There were five of us were good mates, me and the four Cash brothers. The place was so rough, full of banks and hills and muck. Come winter time when we needed to get off site we had to wade across the stream and I was forever falling in and cutting myself. The power station was just behind us and my mum used to send us to there to pick coal in the big chrome buckets. When the guards saw us they used to chuck coal at us to run us off. We'd jump down into the banks and hide. As soon as they'd gone we'd

be back again. We knocked about on Heath Common, playing football and tig, but it got so boring doing the same old thing. Once a year, at Easter there'd be a fairground festival on the Heath. We looked forward to it for weeks before and would run following cars and motors as they came up to the Common, setting up. We'd be at the fairground day and night and when that went we'd be bored again.

As we started to grow up a teacher, Mrs King, came down on site. There was a double decker playbus and we used to learn to draw paintings and things like that. I went to Sandal Magna school in 1982. My dad used to drop me and my brother off. On the way he'd stop at a bakers and buy us fairy cakes. I liked school but I was bored. Being inside all the time made me tired and sleepy and at playtime we used to go and hide - we didn't want to go back. I was there for a couple of years and then we went travelling. I came back when I was thirteen and went to Manygates Middle for a year and a half. I didn't learn much. The teachers didn't make us. I don't blame myself for that. I blame them. They didn't make us and we always felt left out.

I've lived on this site since I was a small child. It was just a bit of wasteland in front of the power station, full of banks and hills and puddles of water. There was never a toilet or a tap and we had to ask for our water from houses and garages. It was more of a Travellers site then with people coming and going from all over the country, there were about two hundred caravans and chickens, dogs, horses - animals everywhere. There wasn't a proper bridge over the stream, which went over the entrance onto the site, it was always flooding and you could never get across. Many's the car that broke down or got damaged there. You'd see plenty of rats and there are still rats and mice, running around after so many years.

I remember the first people coming down to have a look at the site. Mr Bolton was the first on and as a result of that Derek and his wife Helen moved on the site along with us into a caravan. When they first moved on they supplied static caravan homes for those who wanted them. But they're not what people were used to or wanted. There

Roma Special

was a lot of money spent on groundwork and it seemed to take off for about a year. Then it all went bad. The electricity started cutting out. Different workmen were coming and going, you'd see them one day and then they'd be off with the job still not done. The broken, unfinished sheds were left like broken teeth, like tombstones. It was dying away by the day. Helen had a nervous breakdown and then Derek went so we were without a warden. It was at a standstill and everyone was out for themselves.

A teacher, Mrs King, came down on site from Manygates. She helped people to write letters to the council, but it took a long time for the council to look at the problem and to understand it. People didn't really bother about us. We were shoved to one side. They started to move on it and it started to change and develop. It was a real eye-opener. For a while it was beautiful. Now it's gone to wreck again. People come and go not knowing who is what, everyone keeps themselves to themselves. They mind their own life, get on with their own business. The site's too big, sheds are smashed and broken, vandalised by the kids. It's dark and dull and black looking.

I've been on this site all my life. At the moment it is the worst it has ever been. In the old days it was smaller and everyone knew each other, we'd sit out and tell stories about seeing this and seeing that and all the men would wear flat caps and scarves, it was great. Now it is rough on here, there are different people, different families, people are rowing in public and there is rubbish all over the place. The young ones are not the same as the old ones.

When they did the place up it was like living in a palace. We were asked what we wanted doing, they built us sheds with baths and showers and toilets and electricity, it was lovely. In the old days we had to go out at night to turn the generator off. Now all we have to do is turn a switch, which is magic. We had to start paying rent then but nobody minded because of the facilities we had. Over the last five years though, the whole place has gradually deteriorated.

R267 AWT

People started coming on for short stays and these were the people who started the trouble. They'd come and go with no respect for the site or for the people who lived here. They would leave rubbish behind. The council put skips out, but they weren't emptied often enough and when they got full, people started to put their rubbish around them and then it is never shifted. One Christmas the floor was full of old turkeys and they laid there for six months. The whole place needs cleaning up and we need some strict management. It has become a waste of time to go and complain, it just goes in one ear and out of the other.

I have thought about leaving the site. When the shooting happened a couple of years ago I went and didn't intend to come back. The other sites are stricter than this one though and you can't just pull on and stay. That's why them sites are good and there are long waiting lists to get on them. It's like being in a chain when you buy a house trying to get on them.

I came back here because I've lived here all my life, my mam and dad died on this site and I like Wakefield, it's a good area. It's what I'm used too. There's a lot more crime now, in the old days I hardly heard of any, but now you hear of old women getting attacked and that's all over the place. In some ways I think we are better off these days with the social security and what have you. I can remember being told when I was growing up that if you didn't work you didn't eat, at least now if you can't get work then at least you can get some food to eat. But in other ways, we are much worse off now.

Sometimes when I look out at the rubbish and see all the flies buzzing around I wonder. The rubbish is now spilling out on to the car park by the pub. I can't let the young one go out and play in that mess and with all the dogs around. Every time she gets a little cough, I think it is something to do with the site. I went to the White Towers site at Armthorpe, it was a pleasure to pull on. There was a man there with a horse in a box. The council told him he had to shift it or he was evicted. He moved it. That's the kind of management we need here.

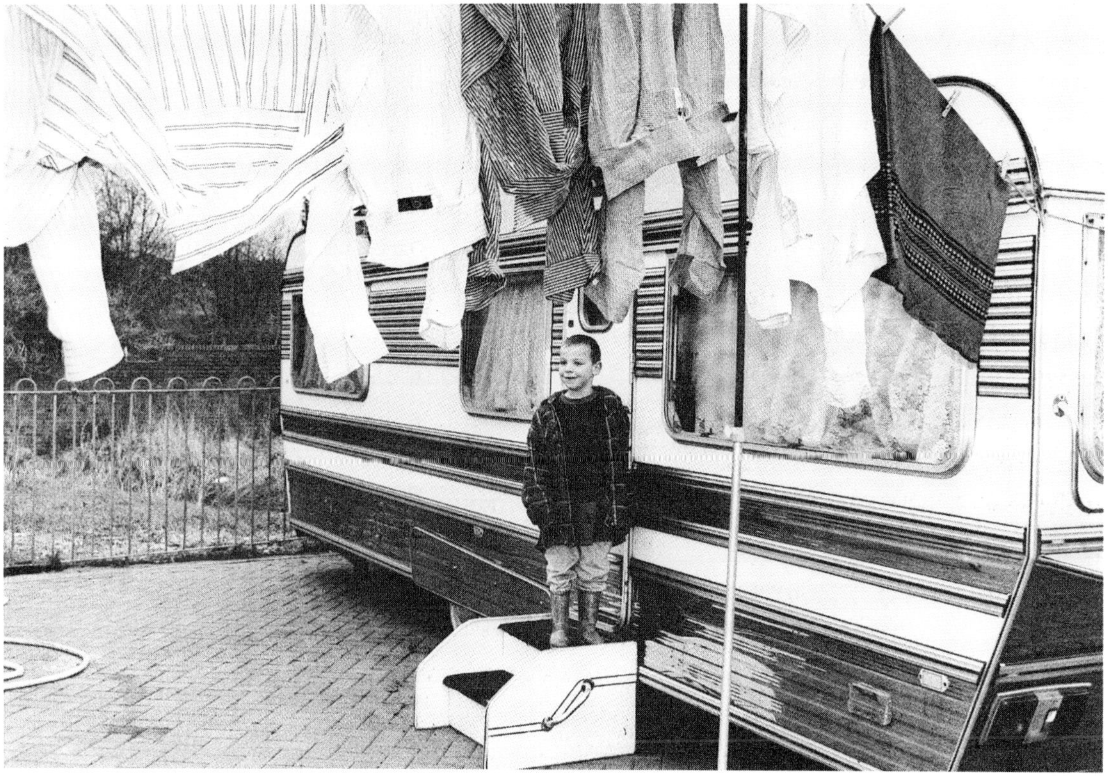

We heard rumours that the Council were going to do something with the site. There were meetings but we didn't always go to them. I can remember that we asked for some things; baths instead of showers. And then it happened. The site got done up and it was beautiful. The Council built the bottom end first and then we moved down there while they did the top. They built stands with sheds on, proper sheds with a bathroom and toilet and a kitchen. The stands were big enough for several trailers. There were planters, with flowers and bushes in them, separating the stands from each other. They put in electricity, made the roads and put in street lights.

For a while this was the best site in England. There was a Tarmac overspill at the entrance to the site where people would pull onto, waiting for a site to become vacant so that they could grab it. There was a barrier at the entrance and you had a card that let you on and off. But there were too many stands and no control of who was coming and going. There was no waiting list, or if there was a waiting list it wasn't kept to. People would pull on and stay whether they were on the list or not. The barrier got vandalised. We didn't know who was here and if there was damage done, or rubbish dumped, you didn't know who was doing it. Summer time one lot would pull off and then you get a load of strangers coming on in winter.

Kids smashed things up. If there were empty stands they would go in and smash the sheds up. People didn't bother about where they put the rubbish. Before if you went to a skip and it was full, you went round to the other side of the site and put your rubbish in the skip there. If they were all full you took it back and waited until they had been emptied. But people were just tipping their rubbish next to the skips and spilling it all over the ground. So the whole site became one big tip. Then there was the trouble. We pulled off before it happened because we knew trouble was coming. A lady on the other side had her windows smashed in when she was away in town shopping. So we pulled off and so did a lot of other people. We were safer when it was a waste ground and we knew all the people on it. No one is comfortable if they are surrounded by strangers who could be trouble makers.

The people in the office help us with forms and read letters for us. They're very helpful like that but they don't know which kids are doing the damage. Things get broken up while they're down there in the office. We didn't want a Traveller running the site, we wanted a gauje. We can't stop kids messing things up. You get more cheek than enough from them if you tell them to stop or they come back at night and smash things up. It isn't enough to have one man. There are too many trailers, it's too big for that. When Derek was running the site there was a council man, Mr Johnson, who used to walk round the site. If he saw kids breaking up the sheds, he'd go to their parents and tell them 'If that doesn't stop, you're off the site'. We used to call him a bad man and a bad man is what is needed.

I think when they designed this site, they designed it for themselves, for what they would want if they lived here. They didn't ask Gypsies what they wanted, so they put in these planters but Gypsies aren't gardeners, they're away and on the move. Kids dig the sand out of them and throw it all over the place and dogs come and do their toilet on it. In the summer you can see mice running around in them. When I lived on a slab at the top of the site with John who had just been born, I could see rats climbing up the walls, coming in from the bankings. The midwife, who was visiting me, said it wasn't a fit place to have children and she was going to speak to a councillor.

I don't think they thought of people with children living here. There are no fences around each slab and the children can run straight out onto the roads. Cars speed up and down here. When they're not at school you have to guard them twenty-four hours a day. Because there are no fences you get dogs coming on to your slab. I have to get up before the kids and clean the dirt up. The slabs should have been made of flat concrete which is cheaper and easier to clean. With these small stones you have to clean in between every crack to get rid of the dog dirt and the kids dig them up. I clean the slab every day as well as clearing the rubbish from the plant pots and cleaning the roads. We have no road sweepers or cleaners here like you would on a council estate.

I was sat having my tea one afternoon, looking out of the window at all the rubbish and flies buzzing around and decided I'd had enough. I went out and started to clear up. Rubbish was piled high and there were thousands of flies. As I was wading through all this I came across a dead dog. I put down my tools and went over to the office. All they could say was that we couldn't catch anything off a dead dog. How true is that?

I have always been a healthy woman, but ever since I've been on this site I've never felt well. Last summer there were loads of cooked chickens in the rubbish. The flies were buzzing, they come into the caravan and land on your food and vomit all over it. It's disgusting. My son was off school for three months, I was taking him down to Clayton Hospital, he was just spewing and spewing all the time. That was from the mess.

The first slab I got on here was number thirty-six. I was given the keys to the shed and when I went in the bathroom, it was covered in poo, not babies poo either. It took me three days to clean that up and when I finished I had septicemia - poison in the blood. They should let the people who run this site live in a caravan on here, then they'd know.

I was once waiting for a letter from the hospital for an appointment with a specialist. I was finally given the letter one Sunday afternoon, the appointment was for the previous Monday. That's no good. I go into the office for my mail, and it's all nice and warm and I ask,

'Is there any mail?'

'Yeah there's loads.'

If post goes into the Royal Mail, then it should be delivered to the person who it is addressed too. We should have our own mail boxes, I don't want people rifling through my mail, opening it and seeing what is inside. Sometimes when we are expecting mail we have to go down to the office everyday to see if it is there. If we had our own box, then all we would have to do is look in our own box, but the postman doesn't come round here. Neither does the milkman, or the dog warden or the road sweepers.

We pay our rent and rates to the council just like everyone else, but we don't get treated the same. I know because I've lived in a council house. I've seen the road sweeper

BITTER £1
LAGER £1.20

come round with the water and the brush and I've seen the dog wardens coming round and picking up wild dogs. I've seen repairmen come round and fix things when they are broken. We don't get treated like that.

There is no excuse for the site being in the mess that it is. There are plenty of good sites to learn from, what we need is strong management. Most of the Gypsy sites are built on old rubbish tips or abattoir sites, most of them I can think of anyway. This site could be a wonderful place, but it's worse than living on a rubbish tip living here.

I've been on this site about a year. I was ill from an operation when I came on here, I'm still sick from it now. When I first came on my shed was in a no good state, the bath was broken, the toilet was broken and it flooded the shed floor. My coalhouse room had bare wires showing where the light switch should be. It has not been fixed a year later.

My grandchild got floored by an electric shock from the wires. A friend tried to cover them up with a bit of cellotape. When we told them in the office, they came over and said it would be alright now with the cellotape on it. I have asked them many times to mend my bath and toilet, nothing has happened. My own doctor even rang up saying that I was sick and really needed to take baths, and that didn't do any good. Imagine getting up in the middle of the night in winter to go to the toilet and you have to paddle through a couple of inches of water on your shed floor to get there. Nobody should have to live like that.

I'm too sick to travel now, so I'm happy enough to live on a site, but I wouldn't want to live in a house with all the burglary that is going on these days. But I'm not used to the dirt, even when I travelled I kept everything clean. This site is a tip, but it doesn't have to be. I know a lovely site in Doncaster, when you move there you are given a brand new electric wire to plug your caravan in, you are given a mop and bucket, a brand new brush and a new dustbin. If you treat people with respect like that, then they will give respect back. I wasn't even given a dustbin when I came on here never mind the rest of the stuff, I had to borrow one off someone else.

I have a burnt out mobile caravan next to my plot. It was burnt down five months ago, I asked them if they would move it, but it is still here. The whole place is a rubbish tip. My daughter brings my grandson to see me, the last twice he has been he has been brought down with poisoning and had to be taken to the hospital. It's a health hazard being here with all the flies and dirt. These flower pots that run down the side of our plots are full of mice. What good can that do? We need proper fences so we can keep ourselves tidy, and if we have a dog, we can keep it in. The dogs are a nuisance here, barking at all hours and sometimes I can't get to the top of the site for them attacking me. The people in the office have one of those electric boxes that frighten them off, if they can't make sure everyone's dog is tied up, then we should have one of those devices.

My sister-in-law lives on Smithers in Barnsley, it's a lovely site. They have a set of rules there, you have to keep your own plot tidy, you cannot cause damage, if you have a dog you have to tie it up, there are no chickens allowed and no outside fires. If you break them rules you are kicked off, and there is a long list of people waiting to get on in your place. That site is beautiful, you won't see a pin on the floor. All we ask is for those kind of rules here and someone strong enough to enforce them, we could do with a good German.

I was born in Dewsbury and when I go away I call this 'back home' and I always come back here. I came back to this site six weeks before Christmas with my four children. The shed is broken, the windows are out and the roof is down inside. There's no toilet, and people have been using the floor as a toilet. I've said to the office that I'm not going in there to clean. It needs industrial cleaning. You don't know what germs or infections are going to be there. They wouldn't clean it out. I've cleaned the slab but I won't touch in there. They said they won't fix the sheds while the slabs are empty because the kids just break them up again. So they want to fill them. The kids take no notice of anyone else and if you say anything you get a mouthful. If you ignore them they go away. But there's live wires in those sheds and kids are in there, playing and pulling things to pieces.

Sex

This site has gone very, very rough. There are motors revving up at night, horns going. It's not the ones that settle here, it's the ones that come on and off. Them in the office won't do anything. On other sites wardens check who's coming on and off and keep an eye on things. I went to visit at Doncaster and when I got back my caravan had been moved. The kids do anything, their mums and dads don't care what they do. I had plants outside but the kids kicked the sand all over the place. It's nice to keep your own plot nice, but there's no point in planting flowers here. The end of the site should be closed down. The site is too big, there are too many people on it. If they knocked the middle bit down it could be a play area for kids.

This site is getting worse. It should be harder to get onto but anyone can pull on. You should be checked and on a waiting list. That happens on other sites. On the Barnsley site you have to put your name down and you can only pull on for one night if your name's not on the list. There's no barrier, like there is on the Barnsley site. You can see where a barrier was put in when the site was done up, to be operated by putting a card in. But it was never properly installed or used and now it's been vandalised, the pole's been twisted and broken. There's no waiting list and no control so people can just pull on, break anything or leave rubbish and then just disappear. And because there's no check of who's on here or what's going on, no-one is responsible for what is done. Say someone comes onto a slab next to mine and breaks the window, they don't get charged to repair it so each time the damage gets worse. We have no say who comes on next to us and it can be anyone.

My side of the site is cleaner than the other side and that's because the families have been here a long time, they don't come and go and they clean up around them. There aren't as many vacant slabs for people to pull onto. But on the other side they're coming and going. Sometimes they come just for one night and just dump all their rubbish. Someone has been clearing trees and left all the stuff on an empty slab, just a few feet away from where my mother is. If it catches fire, or the kids set it alight, it could set her

trailer on fire. And when it starts to get warmer it will be a breeding ground for mice and insects.

The place has turned into a tip. They do clear the skips regularly but the rubbish around the tips, where people have just left it on the ground, isn't cleared. There are only three of the street lights up this end working. The others have been shot out.

There should be someone living on the site seven days a week. There's a Gypsy woman that lives on the Barnsley site, and everyday she goes round the site seeing what is broken and what needs doing. And if damage is done, she knows who's done it and who has to pay for it. But they don't know what goes on at night here. They don't see the cars coming in and being cut up and all the other things that go on.

I can look out of our windows and see everything happening on the site, see who's coming and who's doing what. People are always popping in and out. Sometimes there will be from five to ten people. I don't need to plan to go out to see people because everyone's here. We don't plan, we take life as it comes, we live naturally. Gypsies help each other out, not in sharing money, but when they've got trouble in their life. You can't be lonely on here but if you're stuck in a house then you can't see anyone, you're shut away.

I wouldn't mind moving to a different site but I wouldn't live in a house. A lot of Gypsies move in and out between houses and caravans. Around March time they pull out and then they move back into the house again in September or October. I couldn't live in a house. In a caravan you've got one door and you can see who's coming or going but in a house you can't see behind all those doors. I'd be scared of men being in those rooms. I clean the Christian church up once a month or so and I get scared just being in there and that's the house of God. Me granny lives in a house and I stayed with her, I was scared to open the front door even when I should have known it was her because she had called out and told me so. I was so afraid, I thought it just might be someone else.

I'm not typical of Travellers because I hate travelling. I want things to stay the same. People here in the shops and garages know me, they know me by name. I don't have to put up with the racism you get when you're travelling. When you go to a new place you all get treated the same because they don't know whether you're good or bad. I go to this carpet place in Denby Dale and they know me there. I'm a good customer. But when I went the other day there was a Travelling woman there - Irish - and she was carrying on and being abusive. It made me feel embarrassed and ashamed to be a Gypsy. I can see how people feel. And how would they know, without knowing me that I was different to her. So when I go to a new place I have to start all over again.

I don't want to be travelling, pulled up on the side of a muddy road with the kids out in the dirt and cold, no toilets, no water. In summer we pull away for a while but I'm always glad to be home. He's going on saying why can't we shift and the kids going on saying why can't we have a house.

The site's too big - there should be no more than thirty slabs. What I would like on this site is a transit area for the comers and goers and have it separate from the permanent trailers. Comers and goers have no respect. The kids smash up the site and then they leave and it gets put on all of us then. I know they say we've created this state but they're lumping us all together. There are those who are permanent and there are those who are comers and goers. The warden isn't strict enough and I resent that. It's because he doesn't care what people do.

When I was growing up I was made to have respect, respect for my father, my elders, people's property and everything else. Some of the young today don't have that. Some of the young today do more harm than good. Most of the people are decent, but the police will tar everyone with the same brush. The majority of people in these places are good people, but it is a dreadful state that they have to live in. This site is like hell.